4/14 41 LAO12/13

Strawberry hill branch.
strawberry hill branch

A New True Book

WOODCHUCKS

By Emilie U. Lepthien

CHILDRENS PRESS®

CHICAGO

The woodchuck, or groundhog

Project Editor: Fran Dyra
Design: Margrit Fiddle

Library of Congress Cataloging-in-Publication Data

Lepthien, Emilie U. (Emilie Utteg)
  Woodchucks / by Emilie U. Lepthien.
    p.   cm. — (A New true book)
  Includes index.
  Summary: Describes the physical characteristics,
habits, and life cycle of woodchucks, or groundhogs,
and discusses the traditions related to their role in
predicting the coming of spring.
  ISBN 0-516-01140-5
  1. Marmots—Juvenile literature.
[1. Marmots. 2. Woodchuck.] I. Title.
QL737.R68L46 1992
599.32'32—dc20   91-35276
                                            CIP
                                            AC

PHOTO CREDITS

AP/Wide World Photos—39, 43

© Reinhard Brucker—30 (left)

© Alan & Sandy Carey—30 (right), 33 (right),
34 (right)

Chicago Zoological Society—© Mike Greer,
41

H. Armstrong Roberts—© David Muench, 33
(left); © Mick Roessler, 34 (left)

© Jerry Hennen—32

© Emilie Lepthien—22

Photri—Cover, 16; © Leonard Lee Rue III, 6
(bottom left), 25

Root Resources—© Rae Thompson, 13
(right); © Alan G. Nelson, 17 (bottom left);
© Stan Osolinski, 44 (bottom)

Tom Stack & Associates—© Mary Clay, 6
(bottom right); © Joe McDonald, 14, 21 (left);
© Dominique Braud, 29 (left); © Milton Rand,
29 (right); © E.P.I. Nancy Adams, 37

© Lynn M. Stone—10

TSW-CLICK/Chicago—© Raymond G.
Barnes, 6 (top)

Valan—© M.J. Johnson, 2; © Francis Lépine,
4; © Harold V. Green, 8; © Aubrey Lang, 9;
© Albert Kuhnigk, 11; © Michel Bourque, 12;
© Wayne Lankinen, 13 (left), 17 (top right);
© John Mitchell, 15; © Karen D. Rooney, 17
(top left); © S. J. Krasemann, 17 (bottom
right), 44 (top); © François Morneau, 18, 19,
21 (right); © Chris L. Gotman, 26; © J. A.
Wilkinson, 28; © John Fowler, 45

Cover—Young woodchuck feeding

TABLE OF CONTENTS

WHAT IS A WOODCHUCK?

Woodchucks are mammals. They have hair on their bodies and the females feed their young with milk. Woodchucks are also rodents. All rodents have sharp front teeth for gnawing.

Woodchucks are members of the squirrel family. Chipmunks, squirrels,

Prairie dogs (above), squirrels (bottom left), and chipmunks
(bottom right) are all relatives of woodchucks.

and prairie dogs are related
to the woodchuck. In parts
of North America the
woodchuck is called a
groundhog.

Woodchucks are found
in Alaska, east across
Canada, and into the
eastern half of the United
States. They live as far
south as northern Georgia
and Alabama. Woodchucks
like fields or open
woodlands. But they also live
in rocky places and
on the slopes of mountains.

Sometimes woodchucks climb a tree.

They spend their time on the ground eating. At any sign of danger, they escape into their dens. Sometimes they climb a tree.

8

WHAT DO WOODCHUCKS LOOK LIKE?

Woodchucks have short legs and heavy bodies. Their ears are short, and their heads are flattened.

With their heavy bodies and short legs, woodchucks walk with a waddling motion.

Woodchucks' long, coarse fur makes them look even heavier.

Their coarse fur is gray or brown with some rusty brown hairs. Their legs and tail are dark brown or black. Since their hair is coarse, woodchucks have not been hunted for their fur.

Like many other squirrel

Woodchucks use the sharp claws on their front feet to dig their dens.

family members, woodchucks have four toes on each front foot and five toes on each back foot.

Woodchucks are usually about 20 inches (51 cm) long and weigh from 5 to 10 pounds (2.3 to 4.5 kg). Some may be 30 inches (76 cm) long and weigh 20 pounds (9.1 kg). They move slower than other members of the squirrel family. But their eyesight and hearing are keen.

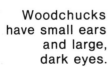

Woodchucks have small ears and large, dark eyes.

Woodchucks have incisors in both upper and lower jaws.

GNAWING TEETH

Woodchucks have twenty-two teeth. Their front teeth are gnawing teeth, called incisors. There is a large space between

13

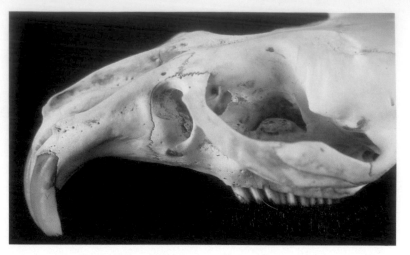

This woodchuck skull shows the large space between the incisors (at left) and the molars.

the front teeth and the grinding teeth, or molars, in back.

The gnawing teeth continue to grow as they wear down. A kind of hinge permits woodchucks to move their jaws from side to side as well as up and down. This helps them grind their food between their molars.

WHAT DO WOODCHUCKS EAT?

Woodchucks are herbivores, or plant eaters. They eat tender green plants, especially grasses

Woodchucks sometimes invade people's gardens to eat the growing vegetables.

15

A young woodchuck feasting in a field of clover

and clover. They also eat roots, bulbs, tubers, and seeds. Unlike squirrels, they do not store food for the winter.

Woodchucks feed in groups. One member stays on guard, watching for an enemy—a coyote, fox,

Woodchuck enemies (clockwise from top left):
Fox, coyote, hawk, and mountain lion

mountain lion, hawk, or
dog. Each animal also sits
up every few moments to
check for danger. Either

17

A woodchuck sits up in the "guard" position.

the guard or a feeding woodchuck will sound the alarm with a shrill whistle when an enemy comes near. Then all of the woodchucks dash for tunnels leading to their dens.

A woodchuck peeks out of its entrance tunnel.

UNDERGROUND HOMES

The underground den is dug below the frost line. Dens usually have several tunnels. Some tunnels may be over 30 feet (9 m) long. Dirt dug from the tunnels may be piled around one entrance. Other tunnels may have been dug from below, and their entrances are well hidden. They are all connected to a main tunnel leading into the den. Woodchucks line their dens with grasses and leaves. The dens are snug and warm during the winter.

If food or water become scarce, the woodchucks move. They leave their tunnels and dens and build new ones. Sometimes other animals move into the old woodchuck homes.

HIBERNATION

In early fall, woodchucks enter their dens ready for a long winter sleep called hibernation.

They are fat from summer feeding. They will live off their thick layers of fat.

In the fall, the woodchucks are fat. It's almost time for their long hibernation.

A hibernating woodchuck curls up into a ball.

Hibernating woodchucks curl up into a tight ball. They tuck their head between their short hind legs and fold their front legs behind their neck. Breathing slows down.

Body temperature drops to between 43° and 57° F (6° and 14° C). During hibernation, woodchucks cannot hear or feel things. It takes several hours in a very warm place to wake them.

Woodchucks hibernate from September or October until February or March. Hibernation is longer in the colder northern climates.

BABY WOODCHUCKS

Woodchucks mate in February or March. About a month later four or five young are born. The babies are naked and blind. They drink their mother's rich milk for the first month.

After a month the babies leave the den to explore outside. They

A mother woodchuck and baby

begin to eat tender
grasses. By July, it is time
for them to leave the
family group.

The young woodchucks
travel only 2 to 3 miles
(3 to 5 km) from where they

A woodchuck family explores the world outside the den.

were born to start their own dens. They dig their dens near food and water.

In spring they will have their own litter of young, and the cycle of life will continue.

WOODCHUCKS AND PEOPLE

Unless they are caught by some animal or shot by a hunter, woodchucks usually live about five years. Some, however, may live for twelve to fifteen years.

Unlike many native animals, woodchucks did not decrease in numbers as forests were cut down.

Woodchucks like to live in farmers' fields and in suburban areas.

As farmers worked the
fields, the woodchuck
population increased. These
hardy animals learned to
eat the farmers' crops
of tomatoes, lettuce,
and other vegetables.

WOODCHUCK RELATIVES

The eastern woodchuck
has relatives that live in
the western parts of North
America. These animals
are called marmots.

The yellow-bellied marmot
and the hoary marmot

The yellow-bellied marmot (left) and the hoary marmot
(right) are close relatives of the woodchuck.

are found in the western
United States, Canada,
and Alaska. Some people
call them rockchucks.

Yellow-bellied marmots
live in the mountains of
western North America.
They live on rocky mountain
slopes.

Yellow-bellied marmots
are also called
rockchucks.

A marmot family usually
has a breeding male,
three to five adult females,
and as many as twenty
young. The colony may
have a territory of 2 to 3
acres (0.8 to 1.2 hectares).
The breeding male may be five
years old before he becomes
the head of the colony.

Yellow-bellies leave their
dens before the snow
melts. They mate within
two weeks after waking
from hibernation. Four

The breeding male rockchuck patrols his territory
to keep other males from taking his females.

weeks later, four to six
babies are born in the den.

In early July the young
leave their den. They do
not grow much the first
summer. So they stay with
their family for a whole year.
The following summer they

must leave.

The hoary marmot lives high up on the mountains. It is sometimes called the whistler because the animals whistle to warn of danger. Hoary marmots have black and white heads

These hoary marmots live farther north than yellow-bellied marmots.

Hoary marmot mother and baby (left). A hoary marmot (right) stuffs itself with tender grasses.

and shoulders. Their backs are grayish white. The hoary marmot does no damage to crops. The yellow-bellied marmots, however, will eat a farmer's alfalfa and other crops.

GROUNDHOG DAY

Throughout the United States, Groundhog Day is observed on February 2. It is part of folklore that woodchucks, or groundhogs, can predict whether spring will come early or late. According to legend, the groundhog wakes up on February 2. He comes out of the den, and if the sun is shining, he sees his shadow. Frightened by his shadow, he goes back into the den. This means there will be six more weeks of winter weather. But if it is cloudy, he does not see his shadow. He stays outside, and spring weather will come soon.

German immigrants brought this legend to the United States. In Germany, the badger was thought to predict the coming of spring when it came out of its den on February 2,

In Germany, the badger was thought to predict the coming of spring. Like the groundhog, the badger lives In underground dens and sleeps during the winter.

forty days after Christmas. In the United States, the groundhog became the animal that predicted spring. By 1898, groundhog societies were formed throughout the country.

A famous groundhog ceremony takes place in Punxsutawney, Pennsylvania, each year. The president of the Punxsutawney Groundhog Club leads a group of people up a hill called Gobbler's Knob. Using a special wooden cane, he raps on a stone at the entrance to Punxsutawney Phil's den.

A sleepy Phil slowly appears. The president

Members of the Punxsutawney Ground Hog Club greet
Phil on February 2, after he emerges from his den.

speaks to Phil in
"groundhog" language and
translates it for everyone
present. He claims that
Phil tells him when to
expect warm weather and
when it will be time for
planting.

Actually, Phil and his mate live in a nearby park. Phil—and there have been many "Phils" through the years—is moved up to a heated den on Gobbler's Knob before the ceremony.

The people of Punxsutawney claim that Phil has never been wrong in his prediction. However, records seem to show he is right about one-third of the time. Perhaps some

Chipper is the official groundhog weather forecaster at the Brookfield Zoo. On this February 2, she sees her shadow.

Phils are better forecasters than others.

Groundhog Day is observed in many places. Chipper lives in Brookfield Zoo near Chicago, Illinois.

41

Children are invited to a Groundhog Day party there. A special "Welcome to Spring" cake made of carrots, honey, and oats is baked. The children sing "Happy Groundhog Day to You." But if it is too cold, Chipper does not come out to greet her visitors.

Groundhog ceremonies are fun. They are a part of American folklore. But groundhog predictions should not be taken seriously.

Members of the Slumbering Groundhog Lodge of Quarryville, Pennsylvania, await the forecast of Octorara Orphy, their local groundhog forecaster.

Hoary marmots (above) and yellow-bellied marmots (below)
often become inactive in hot weather.

Woodchucks—or groundhogs—and marmots have learned to adapt well, whether they live in open fields and woodlands or in rocky, mountainous places. But they fail as weather forecasters.

WORDS YOU SHOULD KNOW

abandon (uh • BAN • dun) — to leave behind; to go away from

adapted (uh • DAP • tid) — changed to fit new conditions

ceremony (SAIR • ih • mo • nee) — a set of actions that is followed on special occasions

coarse (KORSE) — thick and stiff, not smooth and silky

colony (KAHL • uh • nee) — a group of related animals living closely together

cooperate (ko • AHP • er • ait) — to work together to do something

cycle (SY • kil) — a set of events that keeps repeating in the same order

den (DEN) — an animal's home

explore (ex • PLOAR) — to travel to new places to find out what is there

folklore (FOKE • lore) — stories, beliefs, etc., that are handed down among people

forecaster (FOR • cass • ter) — one who says what the weather will be

frost line (FRAWST LYNE) — the lower limit of freezing in the ground

gnaw (NAW) — to chew or wear down with the teeth

herbivore (ER • bih • vore) — an animal that eats only plants, not meat

hibernation (hy • ber • NAY • shun) — a state of deep sleep in which body temperature drops and breathing slows

hoary (HOR • ee) — covered with grayish hair

immigrant (IM • ih • grint) — a person who came from another country

incisors (in • SYZE • erz) — long, sharp front teeth

legend (LEH • jind) — a story from the past

mammal (MAM • il) — one of a group of warm-blooded animals that have hair and nurse their young with milk

molars (MO • lerz) — broad, flat back teeth

native (NAY • tiv) — born in or belonging to a place

population (pop • yoo • LAY • shun) — the total number of animals of the same kind living at the same time

predict (prih • DIKT) — to tell what will happen in the future

Punxsutawney (punk • suh • TAW • nee) — a town in the state of Pennsylvania

rodent (ROH • dint) — an animal that has long, sharp front teeth for gnawing

scarce (SKAIRSS) — hard to find; not plentiful

shrill (SHRILL) — making a sharp, high sound

territory (TAIR • ih • tor • ee) — an area with definite boundaries that an animal lives in

translate (tranz • LAIT) — to tell what someone is saying in another language

tuber (TOO • ber) — a short, thick underground stem, such as a potato

tunnel (TUN • il) — a hole that makes a path down through the ground

INDEX

About the Author

Emilie U. Lepthien received her BA and MS degrees and certificate in school administration from Northwestern University. She taught upper grade science and social studies, wrote and narrated science programs for the Chicago Public Schools' station WBEZ, and was principal in Chicago, Illinois for twenty years. She received the American Educator's Medal from Freedoms Foundation.

She is a member of Delta Kappa Gamma Society International, Chicago Principals' Association, Illinois Women's Press Association, National Federation of Press Women, and AAUW.

She has written books in the Enchantment of the World, New True Books, and America the Beautiful series.